Love Grace & Sorrow in No
Particular Order

Also by Kevin Semeniuk

Collections of Poetry

Love Letters
Hearts of Grace
Tales of Sorrow
In No Particular Order
Revelation

Novels/Fiction

Sweeping with God
Sugar
Grace in October

Fifteen for HOPE Publishing

Cover design by John Pavelich & Kevin Semeniuk
Printed and bound in Canada
Second Print
Fifteen for **HOPE**
www.kevinsemeniuk.ca
Love

Love Grace & Sorrow in No Particular Order

Kevin Semeniuk

Fifteen for HOPE

LOVES' WHISPER

There's a love on my breath
That breathes gently my name
It whispers softly a secret
On how my world you have changed

LOST SMILES

In a part of the world where smiles get lost
Where hope has very little purpose
And dreams are only meant for sleep
It's second nature to feel worthless
Wearing mostly only dust and tears
Playing catch with old grenades
Watching fire fights light the skies
As the burning sun begins to fade
A hunger for life so intense
It sends starvation out on the wind
With a sweet tooth for fresh water
A passion for God helps them play pretend
Permanent dents in mother earth
Where daily they take a knee to pray
Thanking the lord for the air they breathe
Then asking to rise another day
Every day is another shot at life
Just not the kind that comes from a gun
For them it's life they long to live
And for the truth they pray will come

ONE

Let me kiss all of your imperfections
Each little spot that you don't like
Each little stamp that God has given you
Each little corner that needs some light
Let me help you feel safe within yourself
Allow me to love every inch of your being
Inside and out and from top to bottom
Let me change everything that you're seeing
You are perfect in every sense of the word
From your lips to your thighs to your bum
From head to toe frontwards and back
You are beauty in the word that is ONE
O-only one of you will ever exist
N-never again will there be another you
E-eternity will prove that you were on purpose
And I love you for all of this truth

Mom

A life without my mother is scary
It's a fear I choose not to see
I would most likely prefer to go first
In fact maybe I'll make that my plea
I will wander this sad world aimlessly
In search of a love that could match
The comfort that my mother gives me
Is like an old record without a scratch
The sound of a voice filled with memories
The places the times and the smiles
All of the laughs the talks and the tears
Within my heart I've got these in piles
Stacks of smiles and hugs from love
From the most selfless woman on earth
There's nothing I could do wrong in her eyes
I'm so thankful love had her give me birth

BRADLEY

From the bottom of my heart
And from deep within my soul
My one last wish is for you to know
It is your love which kept me whole
I'm forever thankful for having you
To stand strong along my side
You never gave up on me or my life
And not once did fear make you hide
As great of a gift as health may be
It is love that helps us survive
There has never been a shortage with you
It is only your love that kept me alive
I'm sorry for having to leave everyone
Please know that this isn't the end
It's a fresh new beginning for all of us
So I beg you to let your hearts mend
As big as this loss may feel for us all
Please know I am not far away
I have found my sight and my smile again
And I am able to run freely and play
We have a bond that will last for eternity
I am your angel now as you have been mine
I am also okay so you can breathe easy as well
Please don't ever not let your life shine

A Smile or Two

I think I owe you a smile or two
Just a smile or two upon your lips
Because your eyes have kept me smiling
And I am blessed within their grips
There is a special place in my heart
Where I go when times get tough
My own little corner of sunshine
When the darkness becomes too much
It is your smile that is my sunshine
And in debt to you for life I am
Your smile is my sweet treasure
And will surely be so far past the end

LOVES' VICTORY

Standing in a line
Holding her daughters' hand
Being yelled at in a language
That no one understands
It is foreign to her and to others alike
One thousand women and children
Were stolen in the night
Forced into a car
Sitting on big steel wheels
Screaming down the tracks
Praying a rescue is on their heels
The fence goes on for miles
At what appears to be a camp
And she quickly comes to realize
This is where hatred leaves its stamp
As they're shuffled down a platform
She looks across the way
She sees her husband and two sons
And feels that hope has saved this day
With a gun against her back
Her smile swallows her tears
She's sure that love will conquer all
And she will not live life in fear

GODS' REFLECTION

I lay my heart down at your feet
With my purest and most honest tears
I have emptied my entire being
I stand naked within my fears
Truer words have never been spoken
I am love in its rawest form
I am honest enough to believe in magic
Like a child on Christmas morn
Every time I see your pretty face
I understand why a child dreams
It's a hope that makes anything possible
Inside a love that provides the means
You are like the beautiful smile of God
Everything good in the world in a grin
From laughter to sunrise to a shooting star
You are the cure for our worlds' deepest sin
You are the music to which lovers dance
The sounds that ease a baby's cry
A melody which soothes the soul of a man
And makes him believe in his heart he can fly
You are responsible for life at birth
Nurturing kindness with your sweet heart
A love as pure as the touch of God
Because of you man got his start

FREEDOM TO DANCE

The sleep of forever will come to us all
Whether in darkness or beyond the light
Some will grow old while others die young
Some dead in a battle within they fight
In the breath that you carry you will find me
And in mine I will thank you for yours
As it travels it will find no wrong place to hide
Passing with a smile it holds open doors
The shade is a cool place to pause
Even the sun takes a break while it rains
But beyond the clouds the sky remains blue
Such as the love beyond our inner pains
A bird will find song past its search for life
It will sing simply because it's alive
The song within already exists
To find a better song is not how it strives
Each life that will pass through its time
Possesses its worth in the breath of chance
Just like the trees we pick out to cut down
We all deserve equally our freedom to dance

A SHOT AT LOVE

The smile behind your gorgeous eyes
Is much bigger than that on your lips
I can see some of the pain you have
Heartache has clenched you in its grips
You are beautiful beyond measure
My only wish is that you could see
How important you are to the world
And give your love a chance to be free
Please just let yourself be amazing
Or at least let yourself see that you are
Use all the magic you have in your spirit
And treat this world to your wonderful heart
I ask you to let me be the one
With all the honor I have in my soul
Let me show you the way to forgive yourself
And allow me to give you a chance to be whole
Take my hand and spend some time with me
On top of this beautiful world
We will sleep and dream among the stars
Hand in hand we'll dance dip and twirl

BROKE DOWN

I am right here where you left me
With a broken heart and a beaten soul
I almost wish I'd never met you
It's just too bad you make me whole
I loved you with everything I had
Maybe even more than I thought I could
I'm so sorry that I let you down
If I could change it I swear I would
I never knew that you'd outgrow me
It never even crossed my mind
You were the most perfect thing in my life
You gave me sight when I was blind
Now back under the blankets
Is where I'll reside for a week or two
Or until my heart can heal itself
And I find the strength to make it through

PURPOSE

I laugh mostly when I am alone
And I share most of my smiles with me
I sing when I hear a song I like
Mostly 'cause it makes me feel free
I don't always recognize myself
When I wake up and wash my face
The reflection is sometimes odd to me
Like a stranger from outer space
I haven't heard a lot about love
In this life that I have lived
But it is in some of the songs I sing
And I think it's something I'd like to give
I'd like to be warmed up with a hug
By someone who can see my heart
I'd like to be the definition of somebody's love
To somebody who won't let us part
I want to be the reason to not give up
And I'd like to be worth fighting for
I feel like the smile I keep for myself
Should be shared with someone I adore
I want to find the purpose for my life
And share the air which feeds our love
To give away the rest of my laughter
To someone I spend my nights dreaming of

INCOMPLETE

From the darkness I raise my head
Only to see that the light is gone
My heart was torn into pieces
When she said that she's moved on
Her smile was like my sunshine
It was the lifeline of my soul
I never knew that I wasn't complete
Until I realized that she made me whole
Her eyes were like the stars for me
They guided me home when I was lost
But now she's gone and I am stranded
Helpless as a flower on an early morning frost
It is only love or luck that will save me now
From this dark and cold place I am in
I watch the clouds trying to count the days
But I'm not even sure how long it's been

A Beautiful Gift

You came into my life unannounced
With anything but love on your mind
Your heart was still really broken
From what you had left behind
I had never been in love before
And I'd lost my smile along the way
Everything I had been fighting inside
Completely changed for me that day
I had never seen such truth in beauty
Or such warmth within a smile
I could see your heart behind your eyes
I think it was hiding there for a while
I wanted to hold on to you forever
And to be the last boy that you kissed
I wanted to give you all of my tomorrows
And most of all eternal bliss
I would have stood out in the rain for days
To catch a glimpse of your sweet smile
Your beauty has changed the way I look at life
Just knowing you exist makes life worthwhile

DAD

I just want to say thank you dad
If you can hear me from heaven
This is your third born talking
It is me your son Kevin
I felt your presence last night
As I was lying in bed
My heart was weighed down
Then your face popped in my head
I just want to say thank you
If for me you ever lost sleep
Or when I'd cry as a child
In your heart you would weep
I just want to say thank you
For times I was on your mind
Or if for me you would worry
That I was being treated unkind
I just want to say thank you
For being the man that you were
For every second you loved me
I loved you more I am sure
I just want to say thank you
For every lesson you taught
For even the hard ones
Have sure helped a lot
You told me "Thanks for the water"
The last time that we spoke
I said "See you tomorrow"
But you never woke
So I'm here to say thank you
For every minute we shared
For every time that you listened
And every second you cared
I will love you forever
In fact for longer I think
You rest deep in my heart
And I see you whenever I blink

EXHAUSTED

My eyes are so tired
I can't see anymore
And my spirit is broken
With my heart on the floor
Stolen from a world
In the bright light of day
With six other dreamers
Gone to live another way
Forced into a life of shame
Where my body is the prize
I am my parents' lost child
But I'm also someone else's lies
Will I live to be free again
Just to hug my mom and dad
To let them know how sorry I am
If I have ever made them sad
I've become an object of desire
And a slave to filth and greed
I spend most of my time crying
Or praying to God to hear my plea
I have needles put in my arms
By the man who took my life
He says it's supposed to help me
Stop cutting myself with a knife
Marks are bad for business
I'm supposed to be young and pure
And he said that if I stop making money
Then for my life he'll find a cure

SMILE

You've taken me home
Where my smile sits waiting
It's ready to be worn
No more contemplating
This thing that you do
When you touch my hand
It makes my whole body numb
And I can barely stand
I made a promise to love
Before I went to sleep
To never let you down
Or ever make you weep
With you my smile rests
For more than my forever
It won't wake for no one else
For that it is too clever
My smile knows your voice
It loves the honesty you speak
When you whisper in my hear
It sneaks out for just a peek
You make my smile comfortable
In even the busiest of rooms
You're the sun that warms my heart
You make my smile truly bloom

A Time for Change

Where would our world be
And how far into war
Would we continue to murder
And find hate in our core
If we sent out our children
To deliver the news
To every loved one of a life
That we decide to refuse
Of a future here on earth
Instead to die for a cause
In which the suits on the hill
Who ignore half our laws
Say fighting these fights
Will end up in peace
Not only for us
But for all who retreat
To a power that is craved
Over reason or hope
While all these same cowards
Portray their lives pure as the pope
Surrendering to the pain of loss
And the loud screams of fear
With a heavy silence from death
Ringing out in our ears
Send the suits from the hill
To go fight for their cause
While we enjoy peace back at home
From the hill sharing in applause

SOUL FOOD

Would you feed my hunger if I was starving
And you knew I would not survive
Because that's how I feel about your love
Like it helps to keep me alive
Saying goodbye even just for a moment
Does nothing good for my soul
And as my heart catches wind of your absence
It quivers knowing you make it whole

In Session

Imagine if we all stood up
On our very first day of school
When the teacher asked what we wanted to be
We each said "A hopeless fool"
To grow up working as hard as can be
At jobs that we didn't really like
Paying lots of bills for things we don't need
And doing it mostly just out of spite
Being angry a lot for no reason at all
Falling out of love just mostly because
Or maybe it's because we're too occupied
With the future or how everything was
Today suddenly stops being good enough
All of a sudden we need reasons to smile
We stop dreaming because there isn't time anymore
We ignore our hearts and live life on a dial
Going in circles wondering how we got here
Getting depressed about anything we can
Looking for reasons or people to blame
And completely stop being our own biggest fan
The words fun and excitement become only words
Any good feelings are more of a treat
We make it so it's just easier to be broken
So it's less painful when we feel like we're beat
As children we feed off of hopes and dreams
And then along the way we let others mold us
Somehow we just lose sight of ourselves
Being more content to ride the back of the bus

WOMAN

Tell me that I am beautiful
And that you love me as I am
Kiss me softly on the forehead
When our day comes to an end
Tell me how important I am to you
So that I don't have to guess
Whisper in my ear "I love you"
Tell me I'm stunning in that dress
Hold me in your arms and dance
Open doors and hold my hand
Let others know that I am yours
For our love please take a stand
Let me be right once in a while
Even when we both know I am wrong
Brush my hair after I have a bath
Rub my feet when the day has been long
Make me smile when I am sad
But have compassion for my tears
Laugh with me and at yourself
And give me comfort in my fears
Understand that I can be fragile
And that I'm not always sure why
Have patience with my heart
And please encourage me to fly
Take care of me when I am sick
The same as I would for you
Be thankful when I cook a meal
Even if it tastes like an old shoe
Let me know that I am amazing
Especially in the way that I love
Be grateful for every moment we share
For you are the only one I am dreaming of

An Angel Lost

Walking out into the woods
With her solution in her hands
It wasn't but ten years ago
That she could barely stand
Home is not a happy place
And neither is her mind
She's sure that she just isn't loved
And her smile she cannot find
It has been missing for far too long
How come no one else can see
That the pain she has inside her heart
Would bring the strongest of man to his knees
As she takes her last tiny steps alone
She quietly prays for someone to care
To stop her from what she's about to do
But sadly there isn't anyone there
How can a baby understand the end
When the beginning is all they need
Why is a child not loved enough
Why should a baby's heart ever bleed
She strung up a rope with the hope of life
But a life that doesn't know pain
Alone in the woods she took her last breath
And forever our world has been changed

LIES

The poison on your tongue
Burns the truth out from my eyes
And all belief I had in love
Goes up in flames with all of your lies

BELIEVE

I believe in the struggle
That hides behind a smile
And I believe in the love
That's been rained on for a while
I believe in the darkness
That comes before the light
And I do believe in peace
But it's not within a fight
I believe in the dreams
That make a child dance
And I believe in the kisses
That forever breathe romance
I believe in the wishes
That save the lives of love
And I believe in the freedom
That is sent down from above

KISS OF FREEDOM

She must have been an angel
'Cause she had freedom in her kiss
When she pressed her lips upon my cheek
I got back every wish I had missed
Her smile was so pure and perfect
Like falling in love for the very first time
Like when a new mother cradles her baby
The whole world comes together just fine
Her eyes were as deep as the ocean
And held the magic of all the stars
Along with the most beautiful melodies
That soothed the spirits from near to far
Her flowing hair was like the perfect breeze
On the most beautiful summer day
Like when the sun has just finished shining
So that the moon can come out to play
Hearing her voice was like a welcome home
Like a warm embrace from someone you love
It's as if I was lost and didn't even know it
And she was my angel sent down from above

INSIDE A BOX

Most of my life belongs in a box
But I keep my heartache on my sleeve
My forever will be no different
This is only what I can believe
My world hasn't proved me wrong
And mankind just never fails
Whenever a neighbor is doing well
We suck the wind out of their sails
Flushing poison through our bodies
And through the minds of all our youth
Ignoring every single symptom
Just skimming the surface for the truth
Our homeless are heartless villains
At least that's how we're led to perceive
That a man without a home or job
Must not be man enough to bleed
Life is a battlefield anywhere you turn
Just a race to the next green light
Our waters are drowning in greed
We're searching for peace inside a fight
Heaven must have locked its gates
Because earth is overflowing with sin
Tearing down the dreams of love
Just to say the words "I win"

HOPES' FROWN

Standing out on the rooftop
Waving a white sheet side to side
Tied around a branch he found
The walls below him give nowhere to hide
Pain and chaos surround him
Finding no one to answer his call
The price he pays for standing for hope
Has left him alone on his roof feeling small
Falling victim to prayers for peace
Unanswered cries for the sun to shine
The beauty of breath has lost its calm
No longer is love welcome to keep him fine
A soft voice from the ground beneath him
A gentle whisper to call him down
Peering over the edge he sees his son
Seating a smile where once sat a frown
Pulling his love up onto his platform
He hoists the little one up on his shoulders
Handing him the flag to wave back and forth
Together he says their hope will break borders

THE MOST BEAUTIFUL WHEN

To me you're the most beautiful when
You're in your comfy sweats and shirt
With your hair pulled back behind your ears
It is with only you that I wish to flirt
I love it when I get to rub your back
And hear you drift off into sleep
I try to imagine what you're dreaming about
I wish so bad that I could have a peek
To me you're the most beautiful when
You have just gotten out of the bath
With a towel hugging every one of your curves
And drops of water trickling down their path
I love it when I get to brush your hair
As you snuggle down in front of me
Nestled in between my legs you sit
It is these moments that set me free
To me you're the most beautiful when
You share your hopes and your dreams and fears
Or when you're vulnerable sick or sad
And I get to kiss away all of your tears
To me you're the most beautiful when
You are standing or just sitting still
Speaking or not so much as saying a word
To me it's all beautiful and you've broken my will

Lost Boys

Standing at attention
With a gun across his chest
He has no love or freedom
Not even a smile at his best
He lost all belief in happiness
At the tender age of four
When his mother traded him for crack
And sent him packing out the door
Swept under a rug
Until he could hold a gun
Building up strength holding rock-filled sacks
While being kicked around for fun
Just a few months later
Playing lookout on the roof
Down below was a daily war
And not a soul was bulletproof
Fed only by hunger from his hate
For the love that let him down
Now he's pushing dime bag weight
And can't even muster up a frown
Given the chance to feel his heart
And what it's intended to do
This poor lost spirit of a boy
Could heal the soul in a worn out shoe

RIVER OF LOVE

I went to drink from the river of love
But when I arrived it had gone dry
So I bent down on my knees to pray
And beg for forgiveness for all of my lies
If ever I have stepped on a heart
Paying no mind to the pain one may have
I will work for the rest of my breathing days
To bring a smile to those who are sad
My soul dances to the thoughts of love
My spirit whispers its beautiful song
Tickling melodies between my ears
I know now it is for love my heart longs
My lost tears have found their home
Forming a flow on the ground beneath me
As I plea aloud to drown my life in love
The river rises beneath me and sets me free

YOU

You're the kind of love I dream about
The kind that interrupts my day with a smile
You make me believe in a hope so powerful
Questioning who I am as a man all the while
A love so true and pure to speak of
Even my words sit back and listen
To hear the song as you're spoken of
Filling any holes that a soul may be missing
You're all the greatness of a woman
With all the promise of a man
A beauty so strong it makes me weak
Sharing the magic of earths' great span

Innocence Lost

Holding up a sign
Saying "Please Help the Poor"
She's a twelve-year old girl
In which the world came to ignore
The mother to a life
Of a child not yet born
Already crying out for help
And being pricked by heartaches' thorn
With her trust put in a man
Who her mother chose to love
He made her step into the ring
And he didn't use a glove
Now forced into a life
Where she's always on the run
She eats for two from scraps
In search of a hope to have it undone

SHADOW

He sits alone crying at night
For all of the loss that he has had
He searches his mind for better times
But can't find a moment when he's not sad
Upon waking the next morning
He pulls himself out of his bed
Forcing his heart to carry on
He shakes the cobwebs from his head
His shadow is slow to follow him
Passing the window in the hall
It disappears for just a second
Then casts its black along the wall
The two of them start their day off
Just like so many days before
He stops in the kitchen to eat a snack
Before joining the world outside his door
Hopping from side to side behind him
As the light shifts within the streets
Trying to keep up and not miss a thing
It is within his head that his heart beats
His shadow is the encouraged one
Dodging cars and stomping feet
There is no fear in his shadows' life
But for him it's constant defeat
He walks along with his trailing companion
Keeping his focus on the ground
He catches a glimpse of his shadow dancing
As if to the music of the city's sound
Slowing down for the street lights ahead
He stops for a second to think
His shadow catches up beside him
Then he looks down and gives it a wink
He takes off running like never before
In hopes of beating his confident friend
Laughing out loud and taunting the ground
He's found a way to let his life mend

BROKEN

I turn the lights on
Then lay down for bed
It gets darker and darker
As you enter my head
Thoughts of you leaving
And not saying goodbye
You took your love and belongings
With no word of why
I can still smell your hair
As I roll over to sleep
In a bed full of memories
Slowly my heart starts to weep
You were the breath of my life
And the reason for my smile
It's so hard to go a day
How will I ever last a while

LOST IN DEFEAT

Can't you just look at my face
And take a look into my eyes
Can you not see that I am broken
And it is you that I despise
You throw me to the floor
And call me names I won't repeat
You've made our children witness
As I lay crying in defeat
What happened to the love we shared
Why are you always just so mad
I've run out of all my tears to cry
You've robbed my heart of being sad
My smiles have gone and disappeared
And the sky is no longer blue
I haven't felt the sun in months
And this is all because of you
You are a coward and a monster
Yet I'm the one living in a cage
I will continue to take the pain of your strikes
To protect our children from your rage
How much longer will this go on
Before I just up and run away
I wish you'd stand up and be a man
Not cry and beg for me to stay
You tell me you're sorry and that you love me
And that you need us in your life
I know the kids do need their dad
But not to see him beat his wife
One last chance I tell myself
Is what I'm going to give to you
The only thing I'm not sure of
Is if to myself I am being true

A Dreamers' Chance

All he wanted was some change
And to spread the word of love
For peace to find an answer
Before he moved on up above
Hate will always have a presence
In the souls that drown in fear
Until they come to realize
That there is truth within a tear
Hope is nothing but a burden
To a mind that won't let go
But to a heart that's open wide
Many colors it will show
Within hope there's no defeat
This was something that he knew
And no matter how much it rained
Sure as life the sun shined through
Don't judge a man you haven't prayed for
And be willing to extend a hand
Ignorance is the seed of disbelief
For a dreamers' chance is why we stand

FLICKER

Love is no stranger to your voice
You speak of it with every word
Even when your lips are sitting still
You breathe a beauty like I've never heard
Within your eyes you share a dance
Some of the finest steps to be seen
And as your sight may well with tears
You shed a truth which has never been
Your laughter is the song of angels
With not a single note out of tune
Your smile is a reflection from heaven
Bearing a glow that gives comfort to the moon
You are the flicker of a candlelight
In a room where darkness has lost
The whisper on a soft passing breeze
Sharing a secret with my soul at no cost
You're like the comfort of every mother
To a single child who's lost their way
The magic within a baby's first grin
It is with you that my love will stay

NUMB

You put the bottle to your lips
And then you want to talk
Your mouth begins to run
But your words slow to a walk
You feel like it's the answer
To hide the pain that's in your heart
Not knowing that the truth
Lies way back at the start
Your parents never loved you
At least not to your face
They treated you like garbage
And it's the reasons that you chase
Your words begin to fade
As your pain starts to show
And you begin to make it clear
What you want no one else to know
You hurt so much worse
Than words will ever explain
So you continue to use the bottle
To release and numb the pain

TIN CAN

The clanging of a tiny pebble within
Shaking a can and mumbling words
The softness of his voice in screams
Belting out plea's in order to be heard
His travelling companion by his side
With a bronze bell around his neck
The only love he's been shown in years
Is from his old crippled dog named Speck
He speaks words of God and freedom
In a manner not selling a thought
The words he chooses to sing aloud
Are as if specifically it's him they sought
The freedom in which he chants about
Is one that seems to be at our fingertips
It's simply the kind that was born in our heart
It doesn't entail any tanks guns or ships
The God whom he speaks so highly of
Is not the one that may pop up in your mind
This God that he so gently refers to
Goes by another name that is Love you'll find
No sight to witness the absence of a crowd
He continues his souls' request
Speaking on behalf of hope and love
It is for this day that he knew he dressed
The moments of time slowed joyfully
As he heard voices come together by chance
In an instant as if magic had some say
A crowd gathered he sang and they danced

FOREVER

I want to be the last song that you hear
And the last song that you sing
The one that rests forever in your ear
Your hearts' one and only fling
I want to walk with you among the clouds
And share in loves' eternal dance
I want to kiss away all of your tears and fears
And give you never ending romance
I want to be the one you can't live without
Because you are that for me
And I will make sure that you never doubt
Having your heart choose my love as its seed

SHATTERED

Please can you just tell me
What it is that I did
To deserve a broken heart
When I am just a kid
You were blessed with the trust
To watch over my life
But you killed me instead
Without a gun or a knife
You choked the life out of me
And smothered me with fear
I have no one to understand
No one is close enough to hear
I will now live in the shadow
Of who I am supposed to be
Of who I once upon a time was
And I am barely just thirteen
If I am such a special child
Like all those times you had said
Then why would you ruin me
And force me into your bed
I don't get another shot at life
This is the only one I had
Because of you for the rest of my days
I will feel broken ashamed and sad
You have stolen all of my dreams
Just to replace them with nightmares
I sleep at night with my light on
For the darkness I cannot bear

BROTHERS

So very hungry for some food
And starving for some love
Their bodies getting weak
They kept warm within a hug
Spending nights under the stars
And days out on the grind
Always in each others' sight
Kept peace inside their mind
Searching for a better place
Where laughter was a first
Where love seemed possible
As was water for their thirst
Two twelve-year old boys
Who happened to be twins
Have lost their mothers' love
Along with both their grins
Their father disappeared
Which was only for the best
His heart had drowned in booze
When their mom was laid to rest
Lost inside a world of sorrow
With only heartache now to trust
They're strong within each other
But being saved is still a must

Undercover Angel

She could put a stop to war
With the love within her eyes
And the blessings on her breath
Could heal the world of all its lies
She's an undercover angel
Hiding her wings beneath her dress
Here to spread the word of love
And clean the world of all its mess
Sent down from God himself
To do the work that we need done
She sits deeps within our hearts
From her truth we cannot run

LONELY TEARS

These tears I cry are lonesome tears
Parting ways crawling down my cheek
My tears are alone and lost as well
But it's my tears which truly speak
Is it true that love saves lives
Is that why I'm in such despair
My poor love has lost its answer
Which my broken heart has yet to share
It is life which has broke my heart
Although I do not blame my breath
For it continues to give me hope
Sharing dreams with me while I rest
The true love of my life is love itself
But we've been playing this tug of war
Pulling and pushing each other away
Burning my soul down to the core
Love makes me so uncomfortable
It makes me second guess myself
But I long for those indications
Telling me love picked me off the shelf

A War of Her Own

Sadness became an infection
That just would not go away
She spent most of her time crying
And her tears just wouldn't stray
Sleeping most nights on the floor
In a puddle of red wine
With broken dreams all around her
It's quite clear she isn't fine
Gripping love notes in her hand
From her husband who's at war
They're supposed to give her hope
When hope feels like it's a chore
One letter for every day he's away
Is what he left behind for her
With poetic words expressing his love
For every time she isn't sure
She lay sleeping drowning in moments
When they were together in body and soul
Remembering how complete she used to be
For with him she always felt whole
She wakes up and clears her mind
Cleans the mess and wakes the kids
She's at home fighting a war of her own
While her loving husband is off fighting his

My Wish

I wish I could've watched you as a baby
And to be a witness to your sweet smile
To see you roll over onto your tummy
With love in your eyes all the while
I wish I could see you crawl along
And to watch you find your feet
To see you jam them into your mouth
As you begin to fade off into sleep
I would've loved to see your first step
But I would hate to see you fall
I'd love to watch you Christmas morning
As you received your favorite doll
I wish I could see you running free
Without a care in the whole world
To watch you hug your mom and dad
And to see them love their little girl
I wish I could be there to protect you
Whenever someone hurt your feelings
I wish I could be every crush you had
I bet you had boys dancing on the ceilings
I wish I could be the first kiss you remember
I also wish I could be your last
I wish I could be the first you fall in love with
I wish I was your future as much as your past

RECKLESS LOSS

Out in her front yard
Playing catch with a friend
She caught a bullet in her lungs
Which brought her breathing to an end
It wasn't meant for her
But for a man across the way
And as her fathers' heart needs answers
No one has anything to say
As heaven has gained an angel
Planet earth has lost a queen
She was a baby of just nine-years old
Who won't even see her sweet sixteen
With guns being sold in candy stores
And hatred on the rise
Every minute of every single day
Another innocent human dies
Is it not bad enough to lose a loved one
Through sickness or through age
Now our babies have to play outside
In a big steel bulletproof cage

LITTLE MAN

Sleepless snuggled down next to his mother
With holes in the roof to watch the stars
No blanket to cover his tiny bare body
Wishing for dreams to come from afar
His baby sister between him and his arm
With her warm breath against his side
As her tummy moves up and down
The sounds of hunger have nowhere to hide
Echoing within the walls of his soul
Are cries for hope and help to come
With his tears quietly finding their way
To a place of less pain than where they are from
Visions are shared throughout the days
Mixed with smiles to pass the time
A love-filled false sense of freedom
A painted story to make him think he's fine
He understands now the truth of his life
As birthdays have given him years
He's caught on to his mothers' tricks for pretend
Which now assist in his sisters' fears
Never sharing a doubt from within his heart
He allows the smiles and laughter to win
For certain he's sure life can be only this
So he adds to the tales for his next of kin
Little Man is who he is known as
A seasoned dreamer of five-years old
Helping to make the struggles of truth
Become blankets for the tales that are told

COME FIND ME

I beg of you come find me
I am lost within desire
It is your love that I am seeking
It is your love that is my fire
I can't afford to be your maybe
My heart craves to be your for sure
This is a love I won't give up on
For it many pains I will endure
I want to love like I'm supposed to
I need your eyes to help me see
To view the world through love itself
Will no doubt set my love free
You are my chance to stamp the world
And you are my wish come true
My sweet honey from a flower
I believe my love resides in you
Just hold on to your heart
Please do not let it go
Hold a special place for me
For I will love soon this you will know

A LETTER FOR WAR

I need you to fight for our country
To stand strong within this cause
You might even have to kill someone
So for now put your heart on pause
I may have to ask for more than too much
You might have to watch your friends die
And before I forget I should let you know
Any promises from me are a lie
There is no escape for you in this war
It is a fight with no end near in sight
Peace has no purpose among our vision
This is a darkness with no promise for light
There is also a chance that you may die
Or worse come home with such pain
That you forget who you were or wanted to be
Ending up on the streets left in shame
This is my final request for your duties
Come join our fight for money and power
Let's take over the world and kill innocence
Leaving a path for death to devour

FREEDOM RIDERS

Yes you can bruise my body
But not my spirit or my soul
Nor will you ever break me
For you do not make me whole
You can kick dirt in my eyes
But you will not take my sight
My vision outweighs your hate
My peace outweighs your fight
You can even take my breath away
But you will not steal my song
For it will echo in eternity
More so than all of your wrongs
You can push me to the ground
But still I will stand tall
For hope and love do carry me
And never will they fall
I am sorry for all that you've learned
But more so for that which you teach
I am your brother in change
For that is why my hand does reach

SLEEPING BEAUTY

I don't know if you know this or not
I wake up early to watch you sleep
You're so stunning when you're awake
But watching you dream makes my heart weep
If everyone could love the way that you do
Or have someone like you in their heart
I'm certain that peace would surface for good
It's love like yours that makes hate part
Your eyelids flicker in your eternity
As I play witness to your souls' sweet dance
As excited as I am to have you wake
To watch you sleep I thank God for this chance

SEPARATED BY BREATH

We shared our last conversation
Just twenty minutes before
I said goodnight to you
Then I closed the door
I went back to my life
And you to yours
Then I heard my heart drop
And there you were on the floor
I shouted your name
Which for me would be Dad
But I could see in your eyes
You've left a lot of people sad
I took two deep breaths
Then I gave you one
And I beat on your chest
As if it were a drum
I prayed to the lord
To help me get through
To give your heart back its beat
And put me in your shoes
The choice was made clear
And you were taken away
Onto heaven you've gone
And on earth I will stay

HER AND RUBY

Under the hot sun sifting through trash
Feeding her tummy with crumbs
Seven-years old in a fight for life
Breathing her days upon thieves and bums
She's the girl with the lamps and stuff
Old shoes books blankets and things
She keeps the cute little trinkets for her
Dragging her doll along as she sings
Making up lyrics as she hums away
Words mostly of her and Ruby her doll
How they're going to find their special place
With lots of love and a mom she can call
Her and Ruby sell the treasures they find
Out on the corner of lonely and lost
For strangers it's just a dollar or two
But for friends it's nothing they cost
Mingling with fellow street dwellers
Sharing smiles and laughs out loud
As fast as she could make you grin
She's gone sneaking back into the crowd
Stepping all over toes in her dance
Trading partners with every turn
Not a single man or woman pay notice
Leaving only Ruby to show some concern

DESTINATION LOVE

Would you join me on a journey
To a little place called love
We can take a boat or a train
Or we can fly with the birds above
Within your heart is where I belong
As you rest easy within mine
I want to dance with you in heaven
Inside your arms is where I am fine
Take a walk with me to forever
I'll hold you tightly in my grip
I will save you from any tears
From my love you will not slip
Dream with me for eternity
As we lay peaceful among the stars
Keeping an eye on the earth below
Watching new love bloom from afar
We'll listen to all the songs of love
From the birds to a child's soft voice
When we open our ears and eyes to realize
Within love there's no other choice

POISONED SENSELESS

Has someone come to poison the water
Has our well been cursed upon
Why are our children killing each other
Why are babies dying on the lawn
There is no sin within our love
But sin has pleaded with our mind
Pacing frantic for some answers
Searching our hearts with nothing to find
There's no direction for this madness
A ship in a storm on waterless seas
Like a dog biting a man for beating it
Tested for rabies then killed for fleas
What's the sense for all this loss we endure
Not enough mirrors or fingers to place the blame
So many souls have lost their purpose
Bowing their heads they've died in shame
There's no shortage of pain inside these lives
Getting lost within their hollow love
It must me where misguided angles roam
Fighting for their place they push and shove

HUNGERS' PATH

Sitting cross legged in the dirt
Holding his baby sisters' hand
Wearing nothing but a frown
With no strength to even stand
Watching their mother beat the grain
That will feed them their one meal
While they sit and pray together
Telling God just how they feel
"Thank you our savior for this food
It will quench our thirst for hunger
If you could just bless us with some water
That is clean to make us stronger"
The bugs they have inside their tummies
Force them to watch their loved ones die
This was the case with their father today
It's become so common not one of them cried
A pain so pure it has made them stiff
A life with dreams that do not exist
As their mother watches them sleep at night
Counting blessings from her very short list
Watching their bellies bounce up and down
With every breath that they take in
She snuggles down beside their tiny bodies
To get some rest just to rise again

BEAUTY

When I first laid eyes on her beauty
I could feel the whole world stop then turn
That was the true beginning of my life
It's when I really began to learn
Then she came and sat beside me
With her lips humming a sweet song
My soul caught on right away
As my heart began to hum along
There was a pureness in her eyes
Not even the blindest of man could miss
They witnessed all of the goodness in the world
And saw the pain behind every lost wish
Upon her lips sat a smile
Where only the truest of words are spoke
Our worlds' own path to real freedom
Where the angels lay to rest and then awoke
She held a calming in her voice
That could soothe the fears of any man
It was living proof of Gods' true love
Where only the purest of love can stand

THE LETTER

I never planned on being broken
I always wished my heart would mend
I used to practice my smile in the mirror
So you couldn't tell I was playing pretend
There is something so pure in a tear
That makes everything become so real
And a pain that ensures we're all human
When even we're certain we don't want to feel
It's hard to hide behind jokes and grins
More so when you're lost in a storm
Sifting through memories in search of those
That could help to keep me warm
I lost myself such a long time ago
And it's been hard to live with a stranger
I've been fighting to keep this version of me
But I'm just tired of living in anger
I really do love the world as a whole
And I am sorry for having to leave
I need to find the place that's meant for me
For all who I've hurt in this please believe

BEN

I had just walked in from school
Oh man what a day I had
And right when it couldn't get worse
Out popped a brand new side of bad
My bags were packed and ready
All of my posters were rolled up
My birthday presents still wrapped
And a piece of cake in a plastic cup
Some driver was coming to get me
It was time for me to move again
I never even had any warning
I didn't say goodbye to all of my friends
This was the third time in under a year
That I'm being moved to another home
I don't think I'll take my smile this time
I'm so tired of being all alone
How did this become my fault again
What could I have possibly done wrong
I hope it's not because I got into trouble
For adding a swear word to that song
It was just a word I had heard at school
I didn't even know what it had meant
If I did I wouldn't have said it
I wonder if that's why I am being sent
They said I'm moving across the city
Which takes me further from my brother
He's in another home as well
But they left my sister with our mother
She is being taken away soon too she said
That's what the worker told her at school
I don't even know why any of this happened
I think maybe my mom was breaking the rules
She couldn't keep a job like they wanted
But she still told us she loved us every day
I wonder why that isn't enough for them
Or why my mom doesn't get any say
My mom calls me her little angel
She says I'm a gift from God himself
But if I am such a perfect present
Why do I always end back up on the shelf

FIRST LOVE

I thought of our love the other day
As I watched the clouds pass by
I remembered how my heart broke in two
The very first time I saw you cry
We were both out in the schoolyard
It was the beginning of grade five
I watched that boy push you down
Then he called you a name and ran to hide
The world felt like it stopped for a second
And the only ones in it were you and me
My heart sank as you cried in that puddle
Then I ran over and skinned my knee
I fell down right in front of you
And you asked me if I was okay
My face went red with embarrassment
As my mouth ran wild with so much to say
"Me I'm okay don't worry about me"
As I saw your smile eat up a tear
I sort of felt like a superhero
On a mission to bring you some cheer
We both sat in that puddle laughing
Mostly at me and how I had tripped
I knew in that moment I could save you with smiles
And from that second on my world had flipped

MOTHER EARTH

Trees come crashing down
Upon the hearts within the homes of love
As the traitorous wind blows
Spiraling bodies beyond bound in hugs
Flashes of light from the heavens
As the skies scream out to be heard
Sending a warning upon all of man
Within the tantrum are important words
A message from within dark clouds of tears
Dropping frozen bombs upon the land
Damaging food dreams and shelter
In return for what we've done with our hands
Flowers welt and drown in shame
Knowing the sacrifice of their bloom
For man they are just decoration
To fill the space of open room
Holes drilled deep into the core of our being
Birds slick and stuck among the black sludge
The wings of our dreams have lost flight
Man is responsible for Mother Earths' grudge

A BABY'S PROMISE

I will change the lives
Of as many as I can
With the love that I was made from
It is for peace that I will stand
As beautiful as I am
I have an angel in my heart
And any time I slip or fall
Your love will play its part
The smiles that you share with me
Warm my growing soul
And until the day I learn to speak
Please know that you make me whole

SHE IS LOVE

She talks with a song in her heart
She walks with dancing feet
She smiles with the grace of God
She plays along to her given beat
She puts a face to the picture of love
She puts to test the light of the moon
She warms the soul like the beating sun
She's cool like a breeze in the heat of June
She makes you question your intentions
She's also sure to comfort your pain
She is the lucky ones' claim for love
She'll leave you forever better but never the same
She sets a calming over broken souls
She whispers secrets as she passes by
She leaves behind the song she carries
She is love from the beginning of time

Lost in the Dark

Shake my hand with a prayer
That you have said on my behalf
'Cause I'm all out of love
And it's been so long since I have laughed
You see the sign that sits before me
In black it says "please help the poor"
I wanted to write "PLEASE END MY LIFE"
At least maybe that you wouldn't ignore
I am just a simple man who has lost his way
But I need some help to find my light
I'm afraid I won't last much longer than this
Maybe a little love could inspire some fight
It's hard to live life not loving yourself
It's even harder when no one else loves you
I wish I could go back to being a baby again
When life is so simple and everything is brand new
I had a chat with the lord a few nights ago
Letting him know just exactly how I feel
I told him I'd forgive him if he'd forgive me
Then we could begin a whole new version of real

PILLOW TALK

I want to share my pillow with you
For the rest of my dreaming nights
I will worship you like the queen you are
Pulling down stars to provide you with light
From head to toe you inspire me
With your sweet beauty all in between
I heard you had the sun and moon fighting
Over who'd guide you with their brightest beam
Convinced that you're an angel
Thinking you'd need light to guide you home
Not realizing that angels belong on earth
To protect us when we're all alone
I would fight the sun and the moon
Along with anyone else in my way
To keep you here with me forever
On my pillow until my dying day

MY DAUGHTER

I'm so sorry for having to leave you
I promise I did not want to go
I wanted to stay with you forever
I hope in your heart that you do know
Although I have become a witness
And I get to watch you every day
You've grown into quite a woman
And you're a mom which blows me away
You have done an outstanding job
Of dealing with my absence in your life
I'm above and beyond being proud of you
And now you're going to be somebody's wife
I'm so sorry I missed this day of yours
Along with every missed hug and tear
But I have kept a close eye on you
I miss you so much my daughter my dear
I need you to understand this
That in our lives we receive great things
You are the best I could've prayed for
Because of you my heart still sings
I left you a song inside your heart
With the memories of our time
I see the way you look at your children
That warms my soul and keeps me fine
I hope that you know I am okay
But I am sorry for any pain that I brought
The lessons we learn in each of our lives
Are always more painful than we ever thought
I am happy to see you smile so much
And I love that you're such a good mom
I want you to know that you have my blessing
And forever in my heart you are number one

FOOD FOR THOUGHT

With hopes and dreams in her pockets
And a book bag on her back
She makes the trek to school
On an empty stomach and without snack
Right on the heels of this ten-year old girl
Are her brothers of seven and five
Along the way they laugh and play games
Eating up snow to help feel alive
She kicks a can to help pass the time
And to stop her mind from wondering why
They took her fathers' job away
Just weeks after her mother had died
Weak in the knees from a lack of food
She still forces herself to go learn
Hunger and burden will not hold her down
For a better day her hearts' fire still burns

My Love

There is a magic in your voice
That summons my heart to yours
And whenever words sneak of your tongue
It's proof the true love of God occurs
I can feel the sun from behind the clouds
As it sings a song while it takes a break
While flowers bloom before my eyes
My heart has a promise it needs to make
Never again will you cry out of pain
And forever will I be around
I will follow you until our time has come
And not once will your feet touch the ground
I will worship the beauty and love in your heart
And I will thank God for you every day
For you are the angel who blessed my soul
And it is with you that my love will stay

FALLEN

We fly through the night
With the body count high
As we speed through the sky
Trying to make it out alive
Many are battled
Some just bruised
We look at each other
Thinking how did we lose
So many great men
And so many great women
Their bodies piled high
And covered with cheap linen
With their families back at home
And not yet word of the news
So many fallen humans
How does ones heart ever choose
They say this is the answer
To make the world a better place
How can that possibly be true
When there's human lives being erased

Starving Angels

Digging in the dumpster
Behind the brick wall
He stops for a second
As he hears her world fall
Starving for food
And for freedom for those
Who continue to take
All of life's unfair blows
He runs to the corner
As she lies in the street
The vehicle has gone
And left her heart with no beat
He gets to her side
And is the only one there
As he fills up her lungs
With what's left of his air
He pounds on the chest
Of this mother of two
As she lets out a cough
He takes off a shoe
He props up her head
With his beaten down sole
And as she shares with him a smile
The once broken man feels whole

BEAUTIFUL

Her eyes sing a song of joy
That could heal the heart of any man
And a smile which sits upon her face
Makes you question when life began
There isn't a sadness she could not cure
Or a beaten soul she could not mend
For the love that rests upon her breath
Ensures she's a gift God had to send

BULLIED

They push me in the corner
They call me dumb and fat
They've even spit on me
And laugh when I am up to bat
They make fun of all my clothes
And sing songs about my hair
They throw me in the snow
And steal my lunch for them to share
They say my mom doesn't love me
And I'm the reason my dad died
They even pulled my pants down
When I had no place to hide
They beat me up on Halloween
When I dressed up like a clown
They stole all of my candy
And left me lying on the ground
They tell me that I am worthless
That I'm pathetic and call me gay
My mom says gay means happy
That doesn't make sense for them to say
I have tried to tell the teacher
But she tells me to make some friends
I have but only one inside myself
Will this be how my story ends
Every night I wish for better days
And hope that someone likes me soon
I laugh sometimes underneath my bed
And smile sometimes when I see the moon
I wrote a letter to my mom
Telling her I love her and saying goodbye
I read it just about every day
Or every time I want to die
I think it might be better for me
If I can go to heaven with my dad
At least I know that he'll protect me
And I won't spend another second sad

HOPE

To have a dream of eating food
And to grow up without dying first
To watch our parents just grow old
And to have clean water for our thirst
To stop witnessing loved ones die
From a different kind of sick
To afford to get a needle
That's the world that I would pick
To bite into an apple
And to eat down to the core
To afford to buy some medicine
In case it makes my stomach sore
If love were the only answer
Then I'd live on for eternity
But there is money that is needed
And I live in poverty
I didn't choose this world
Just as you did not choose yours
And all I need is just some help
To pry open some closed doors

A BETTER MAN

Help me to honor my journey
And help me grow into a man
Nourish my heart and listen
By my side please take a stand
I don't know why I'm not whole
But you sure take me closer to it
The truth in my smile is for you
With you I want my love to visit
Emotions don't come easy for me
And my words may fumble and trip
But I need you to know my heart is yours
And from my love you will not slip
I know it's hard for you to trust
As it is for me to do the same
My heart's been broken so many times
I thought in me heartache found claim
Please know that it's a struggle for me
To find that voice that dreams out loud
That little boy inside my soul
Who stops his day to count the clouds
Every day I try to be a better version
Of the me I was the day before
But in this fight to find perfection
I'm losing myself just a little bit more
So I can't promise you the world
Only because the world is yours to have
But I can change the way you see it
And make you smile when you're sad
All I ask is for you to understand me
And to know the truth of who I am
Among the honesty of who I strive to be
For you one day I'll be a better man

A SILENT SONG

Just finished my day as I rinse away
All the dirt and filth from chores
Laid my brothers' heads to rest
On the cold of our clay house floors
As I prepare myself to lay for sleep
I share a quiet prayer with the lord
Thanking him for the air I breathe
Then asking why food feels like a reward
How can my song be heard I ask
If no one is near to hear
If no one knows that we need a chance
How will my voice find an open ear
I pray to you every morning and night
Is there something that I have done wrong
Is it bad to want my parents back
Please God just help me sing my song
Sometimes being alive just isn't enough
When inside alive isn't how I feel
I know you see me cry alone a lot
Please God can we just make a deal
I will continue to raise my brothers to men
And I will never speak work of our talk
Please some clean water and food once a day
God it is for you in my life that I walk
I pray dear lord that I am not out of line
I just hope to one day enjoy my song
With all of the melody you have blessed me with
Maybe one day you can sing along

FAITH

Kneeling in the corner
She started to shout
For the lord above
To come and take her out
Take her out of her world
That has only been pain
Not only for her
But for others the same
She can't fake it much longer
And try not to cry
She's too tired of trying
And wondering why
Just how could it be
That in this day and age
She lives in a world
Filled with hatred and rage
Her heart bleeds with sadness
From a world away
As the lord reaches out
And asks her to stay
She is needed here
To help heal mankind
She's the angel we all have
In the back of our mind

NEW WORLD

Stepping over fellow man
Just to try and get ahead
Watching children starve to death
Sweep those visions from our head
Move along with dollar signs
Chasing other peoples' dreams
Judging those with less in life
Faking smiles by any means
Pushing through unhappiness
Breaking families up with lies
Peoples' new found selfishness
Replaces truth within our eyes
Conversations typed in words
Human contact less and less
Voices saved more so for pain
On how our world is such a mess
Where love was once the answer
In its place now sits a fear
That we must all conform to paths
With little room for joy or tears
Smiling seems uncomfortable
And laughter has become a treat
Passing open begging hands
Makes us angry in the street
Why should we give away our coins
That we work so hard to gain
With such great value in our own struggles
We've gone blind with our own pain

Lost Soul

You walk through me as though I am a ghost
But I am certain that I am not dead
I take a step back into my shadow
To stop and scratch my head
A toque and a torn t-shirt
And holey pants which have not been blessed
The soles worn out on both of my shoes
And weeks since I've had any rest
The love of my life works these streets
She feeds our hunger with her body of lies
But every time her and one of them meet
It is my weakness in which I despise
She is my fix not only for love
But it's only love that she wants from me
I cry out in the darkness in search of answers
Seeking a God to shake this disease
A flame and a glass pipe are now more important
To my body but not to my mind
My heart no longer has a say in my life
But it is my heart that I long to find

A Childs' Plea

I want a hug for no reason
And to hear "I love you" just because
I want to wake up with a smile
Like every happy child does
I need to hear your praise
When I've done something good
And I need to feel your love
If my efforts have been misunderstood
I need protection from the monster
Who lives beneath my bed
And endless understanding
For the fears which rest inside my head
I have potential to be anything
More so if your love is on my side
I need you to be okay with me
To help me dream and be my guide
You don't always have to know the answer
But you can help me find the truth
Invite me to stay up late with you
Make me feel special when I lose a tooth
I am the child you were blessed with
Love me forever and feed my soul
And I will love you ten times more
Because without you I am not whole

BAREFOOT IN FORTUNE

Barefoot and broke he is lost
Nameless to strangers he's found
With his hands out to the world
His eyes to the sky and his knees to the ground
With change in the form of a smile
And some nods from passers by
A handshake from a blind man
The glare of a child who asks of why
Frozen in a time of years gone by
Tracking a smile lost deep in the past
His lips are still with a poetic tongue
Saving his dreams for moments of last
Locked inside a motionless body
Trapped in a fear which makes him resist
Caught in the dark begging for chance
Each tear is a plea to make the lords' list
Saved by the breath in his lungs
Exhaling the love from his polluted heart
The light of his soul shines brightly
Gripping the fortune of a God given start

BED OF LIES

Don't ever say I didn't love you
'Cause I did I gave you me
I gave you everything I had
But you were just too blind to see
You chose to love another
Even for a single night
You called it a mistake
Said you were mad 'cause of our fight
The wrong in your decision
Broke my heart right down the middle
Taking me from someone in love
To feeling lost alone and little
Every time I close my eyes
I see you in your bed of lies
I wish my heart could just forget
But I remind it when it tries
The pain that sits inside my tears
Will protect me from those like you
Until the day I find an honest kiss
One which proves that love is true

CANDY COATED SMILES

She cries with smiling eyes
Her heart is broken in two
She tries to fight the tears
But they push to make it through
Her soul is lost in heaven
Her spirit is gone as well
Her mind is fighting for freedom
While her breath is under his spell
He keeps her light upon her feet
He dazzles her with flowers
Dimly lit dinners and candy
And diamond dripping showers
She wanders in a sightless world
As he watches and speaks for her
The music plays without any words
The writing has become a blur
Tasteless no flavor life's bland
Gold necklace and gold covered hand
Pearls from depths of the sea
Fur coats and heels she can't stand
Two dimples to accent her smile
Brown eyes to make them all fall
Long brown hair and olive skin
She's got them lining up along the wall
Cake in the form of a bill
Some sugar to sweeten the treat
A purse she's got armed with protection
And a shot to numb her defeat
The numbers she carries in years
Possess no questions to those who seek
The goods she handles at work
Makes even the strongest of them weak
She hides the beginning deep in her heart
While she stores the end under her bed
The story she's trying to finish alone
Stops with a gun against her head

CRACKED DREAMS

He fell and he flipped the script
He lost the sway in his swag
He's got a lean when he walks
From all the lies in his bag
He ain't skippin' he's trippin'
From the truth he's been flippin'
It ain't a test it's a lesson
He took for granted his blessings
He has to run to the darkness
Where all his demons he hides
He snuggles next to their shadows
It is with them now he rides
He likes to call for the clouds
He wants the sun to stay gone
He has no room for new growth
He needs his soul to move on
He packs his heat in his pocket
He keeps the flame in his hand
He still kneels when he prays
But just to tie off the band
Gripping the line in his mouth
He bangs his dreams back home
And for a second he's guessing
He's gonna die all alone
He floats freely he's flying
He starts to stagger he's trying
He wants to talk before lying
He wants to live before dying
With the moments he passes
And the minutes gone laughing
His young lungs now collapsing
It is his death now he's trapping
All alone on the floor
His body switchin' and twitchin'
His demons calling him home
But it's for heaven he's itchin'
His heart is fighting for life
His mind is trying to hang on
He shouts out for a God
But now it's too late he's gone

DREAM GIRL

I'm in love with a girl
Who doesn't know I exist
It's that same old love story
But this is one I won't miss
She's the girl from my dreams
The only song my heart sings
She's my souls' deepest secret
It is the purest of love that she brings
The sweet carrier of words
That calm my troubled mind
There's a certain truth to her beauty
That helps my heart to unwind
There is no error in her ways
Her smile is surely built to heal
There is a magic on her lips
That makes everything become so real
I'm going to keep her tucked away
And visit her each and every night
Or until the universe sways in my favor
Making my dreams true to my life

TEARS OF DECEIT

You take my kisses and go
My hugs my heart and you leave me
With my broken soul at my feet below
Even my tears will now deceive me

FADE TO GRACE

I stumbled upon myself in him
As I watched him fade to grace
Without a thought I fell in shame
As the tears rolled down my face
I knew him once some time ago
Passing eyes within the streets
I caught him in a struggle for hope
And now his heart would fight for beats
We parted ways with a handful of coins
From my pocket to his wink and grin
No words to share or time to mend
Trapping us both in the loss of a win
Within the dark of passing time
And no light to shine beyond
I'm on my knees in a prayer for life
That is for his to carry on
I was meant for this to take its course
As I was given the gift of birth
In life I find the breath we share
Lie no secrets to our sacred worth
Moments slip passed our crossing paths
His time has now become mine
My heart will now carry forever his coins
The worth I once placed as I traveled life blind

ETERNALLY YOURS

Standing at her bedside
He holds her dying hand
His mouth is full of questions
But his tongue is at a stand
His lips won't move to speak
But his eyes are full of words
His grip is seeking answers
It is his heart that she has heard
As her eyelids fight for light
The window to her soul has cleared
"What is it my love" she asks
As his eyes begin to shed their tears
"How come I don't get to keep you
For as long as we had planned
Why are you leaving me all alone
Without you I'm just a man"
Her lips soften to a smile
As her cheeks begin to blush
"You know I'll always be here with you
You are my one and only crush"
She pulls his hand over her heart
As he does hers to his the same
They smile and slowly close their eyes
Softly whispering each others' name

WHERE THE SPIRIT LIVES

My heart is gone with the wind
My smile hides in the trees
They took me away from my family
They injected my life with disease
The light has gone out in my soul
My tongue has lost its rights
My eyes no longer see color
Even the days are dark as nights
Trapped in a world of strangers
Lashings to cure my wrongs
My mind is fighting for freedom
I can't hear my peoples' songs
The beat of our drums for miles
The cries of our warriors chants
The light of a fire protecting us
Our stories being told in dance
Force fed daily reminders now
Lessons being taught with pain
For even a moment of cheer
Leaves another trapped in shame
Like dogs they say is how we act
So I find comfort under my bed
The girl beside me does the same
And with our dreams our spirit is fed

So it Begins

You left your dreams on my pillow
I saw inside your world last night
I could have stayed asleep forever
Within the darkness of your light
I kissed my lips upon your eternity
As I lay studying your sweet dance
My heart paused for a second to break
Then doubled its beat in loving chance
I played witness to your vision of love
And to the kisses you'll give to your king
The collision of two souls' secrets
The beautiful song your heart will sing
I heard your smile whisper a name
And as it is so I shall be cast into the wind
For the dreams you've left are not mine at all
Yet my dreams are of you and so it begins

The Kiss

I can taste the love upon your lips
Each little dream nestled in your kiss
As you waken my poor sleeping heart
With the beauty of heavens' eternal bliss

STILL WITH YOU

It's coming up on four years
Since you left me behind
Just in body and breath
You're still strong in my mind
I still miss you the same
The pain just simmered down
I wear my smile out more
I had to trade in my frown
I keep a bag with your things
Next to the bed in my room
With your glasses and cufflinks
And your bible and shoes
I've come to peace with your passing
I keep your life in my heart
I've got your hand on my shoulder
For times that it may get dark
Your name is stuck on my tongue
So our visions get to collide
I get to spit out your picture
With the love I keep deep inside
I see the distance between us
Keeps you waiting on sleep
So you can come down and visit
Once I'm done counting sheep
As you rest close to my soul
While I spend my living awake
You can come journey with me
For the life of our father-son sake

THE BREATH OF LOVE

You were the first breath of my day
After you danced in my dreams at night
The only song that would play in my ears
The only reason my heart found light
You were the friend I found in love
The magical love I found in a friend
I always believed we met before I began
And that we'd hold hands far past the end
I still see you when I close my eyes
You still lighten the darkness in my beyond
My soul shivers in the cold of your absence
Of you I will forever grow fond
It is your tears that fall upon my cheek
Rolling down to the frown of my lips
With the touch of each little piece of you
My frown flips at the thought of your kiss
It is only you I will forever dream of
Only your breath I will forever breathe
As the song of our love plays on in my ears
It is in our love I will forever believe

GONE AWAY

Please come home to me my dear
I beg you please come home
I need your hug and your sweet love
I am broken I am lost and alone
Why did you have to go away
You promised you would be back
You swore you'd never leave for good
And now a father our children lack
I can't imagine what you went through
Or how you spent your last few breaths
It rips my soul to picture you
Lying dead among the rest
I understand this was the job you chose
And in part that it chose you
You believed that you could make a change
Oh my darling I was sure of it too
A soldier a father and a beautiful man
A husband and a lover with a heart of gold
I'm so sad and sorry that I've lost you to war
Forever in my heart your love I will hold

BITTER LOVE

As hard as it is not to love you
I still have your heart in my eyes
I can still taste your kiss on my lips
Even over the bitterness of lies
The crown I once wore has now rusted
The jewels from yours now lay in dust
I was great as your king and you as my queen
Until our lives became subject to trust
I wouldn't trade anything for our love
It is perfect as it struggles for air
I'm not even sure how we can now save it
But then letting go just doesn't seem fair

SHE IS HOPE

She blows kisses to the wind
For any set of lips to steal
She fills pockets and hearts with love
In a world where love isn't always real
Stealing dreams as she passes
Placing breath upon the soul
Filling gaps in human forms
In a time when many are not whole
Mending spirits with her smile
Setting wings upon their backs
Curing fear with all of her light
From a faith that darkness lacks
With a kindness on her tongue
Whispering to the child in us all
She breeds hope belief and freedom
With such a love that will not fall
She is the truth that we are seeking
And the vision that will set us free
The thought behind a war-less world
She is everything we need to believe

FOOLISH

Would it be foolish of me to think
That our love can change the world
Or that the very same smile you wear
Was made to make my heart drop dip and twirl
Would it be foolish of me to think
That your heart was made to heal
Or that the secrets on your tongue
Shed a vision much larger than real
Would it be foolish of me to think
That the music beyond my ears
Is the song of your souls' sweet dance
And is meant to soothe me in my fears
Would it be foolish of me to think
That my breath is that of yours
And that the whispers hiding within
Are the knocks of angels at the door
Would it be foolish of me to think
That your love alone has saved my life
And that the reason for me is you
Now will you be foolish and be my wife

SKIN DEEP

The shade of my skin is a blanket
To cover the secrets of my heart
Deep in a world that disowned me
And from a love that never played its part
The treasure that is me has been lost
Tossed around and shared among men
The belief I once carried in faith
Has been gone since before I began
Born into a world with no hope
And no light to help guide me home
No hugs no kisses no freedom no dreams
No comfort when I'm all alone
I am the difference in color of class
I am the shadow of my youth
I am the dishonor that society sees
I am the sadness that lies in truth
As the sun has rose so I can bloom
And the wind has carried my name
As Mother Earth shed tears for me
Settling the dust that once was shame

LOVE AND CENTS

With her tiny bare feet in the dirt
And streams of tears upon her cheeks
The blowing wind against her face
Blurs the vision of love she seeks
Drying her tears of young sorrow
Leaving the tracks of loss in dust
Her pain from hunger now fading
As her heart has started to rust
No parents to claim for her days
No song to call her back home
No one so close to hold her small hand
Or to lend her a smile when she's all alone
In all of her sadness she is common
She has no certainty to make it to five
There is a hope across oceans and borders
That could prove love and keep her alive
Saved by cents of the human kind
Her little bare feet may be covered one day
But more than that she deserves her chance
To grow up as a woman and visit old age

I AM

I'm a page I'm a story I'm a book
I'm a treasure I am pleasure I'm a crook
I am honest I'm dishonest not by choice
Hear me sing Hear me roar Hear my voice
I am love I am truth I am sight
I am anger I am darkness I am light
I am pure I am tainted I am raw
I am strong I am weak I am law
I am hunger I am haunted I am poet
I am me I am you This I know it
I am quick I am sharp I am clever
I am Life I am Death I am FOREVER

About the Author

For as long as he can remember, Kevin has found his place of peace within stories. Whether it be acted out in movies or snuck in between the melodies of singers from times beyond his years, he's always been sure to lose himself in the treasures of a story, while steadily being reminded by his heart just who he is... a storyteller. Kevin found his voice in a pen at a young age but managed to keep it under wraps under later in life, when he began to share it with those closest to him before branching out into the world of poetry. Although he does hold a strong attachment to his poetry, only a small handful of his writing belongs to his life. Kevin has found a way to connect with the sometimes seemingly overbearing world and give a life of different circumstance a story to be heard. With a nagging belief in hope and the magic of dreams, Kevin has put together his first collection of poetry. The short story rhyming styles of his painted words share a glimpse into the way he views the world; a world of great worth, full of silent images pleading to find their pen.

For any additional work or to simply visit the world through his eyes, you can visit Kevin's website, where he often exposes the bond of hope which he so strongly believes we all share.

35023896R00066

Made in the USA
Middletown, DE
01 February 2019